For my community of Vermont College
of Fine Arts picture book writers
– J. K.

For my awesome parents
– A. B.

First published in Great Britain in 2019 by Simon & Schuster UK Ltd • 1st Floor, 222 Gray's Inn Road, London WC1X 8HB
A CBS Company • Originally published in 2018 by Beach Lane Books, an imprint of Simon & Schuster Children's Publishing
Division, New York • Text copyright © 2018 by Jane Kurtz • Illustrations copyright © 2018 by Allison Black • The right of Jane
Kurtz and Allison Black to be identified as the author and illustrator of this work has been asserted by them in accordance with
the Copyright, Designs and Patents Act, 1988 • All rights reserved, including the right of reproduction in whole or in part in
any form • A CIP catalogue record for this book is available from the British library upon request • 978-1-4711-8254-9 (PB)
978-1-4711-8255-6 (EB) • Printed in China • 10 9 8 7 6 5 4 3 2 1

WHAT DO THEY DO WITH ALL THAT POO?

written by
Jane Kurtz

illustrated by
Allison Black

SIMON & SCHUSTER
London   New York   Toronto   Sydney   New Delhi

At zoo after zoo
the animals chew.
And then . . .

...they poo!

Poo is made of mostly water but also bacteria and bits of undigested food. Animal poo goes by a lot of different names, including manure, scat, droppings, dung, castings and guano.

Giraffe poo looks like marbles as it drops a long, long way.

A giraffe has four stomachs, so it digests its food very efficiently. That means a giraffe needs to eat a lot less than most herbivores, which is why its droppings are so small.

Panda poo is full of bamboo.
Pandas eat and poo all day.

Pandas digest only 17% of the bamboo they eat, and the leaves and stems pass through their systems very quickly, so panda poo looks like a green mass of partly digested bamboo – and it doesn't stink!

A hippo sprays a shower with its flipping, flapping tail.

Hippos use dung showering to mark their territories and warn off predators. They shoot their dung out while flapping their tails to spray it around.

To weigh a day of an elephant's poo, you need a sturdy scale.

An elephant can eat around 140 kilograms of leaves and grasses a day and then dump about 75 kilograms of poo. (To help you think about that, a football weighs just under half a kilogram.)

Rhinos can communicate through piles and piles of scat.

Each rhino's poo has its own unique smell. Rhinos smell dung to gather information about one another.

A lion sometimes buries poo – like any other cat.

Cats big and little often bury their poo so it won't be detected by enemies. But sometimes lions and tigers leave poo unburied as a warning that this is their territory.

Sloths creep down from trees to poo, but only once a week.

Why do sloths spend so much energy leaving the protection of trees to poo on the ground? It's a mystery scientists are trying to solve.

A penguin shoots its poo out
in a fishy-smelling streak.

Penguins don't have teeth, so, as one zookeeper says, "Fish go through them fairly rapidly." Scientists have studied the force it takes for a penguin to shoot its bright-white fishy guano so far.

A wombat's poo is cube-shaped,
so it isn't very roly.

Wombats are highly territorial. They each deposit 80-100 droppings every evening as signposts to say, "I'm here." (It helps to have a square signpost that doesn't roll away.)

Some snakes poo only once a year. They digest their food sloooow-ly.

One study showed that it took a python 5½ days to digest a rat. Because their bodies are so efficient, snakes poo less often than almost any other animal.

Hyenas crunch up lots of bones.
That's why their poo is white.

The calcium in bones is what makes dried hyena poo
white – and why hyena poo can easily turn into a fossil.

Bat poo has undigested bugs –
bats poo all day and night.

Bats turn right side up to do their poo so they don't get any on themselves. A bat can eat up to 1,200 mosquitoes in an hour. Many bats also eat insects with shiny outer coverings that don't get digested, which makes the bats' poo sparkly!

So what do zoos **do**

with all of that **poo**?

A lot goes in lorries to be trucked away.

A zoo might have to deal with more than 2,270 kilograms of poo each day. Keeping it around would make zoos pretty smelly, so some of them pay thousands of pounds a year to send it off in trucks to landfills.

They send some to vets
and to scientists, too.

Then zoo poo is studied to help out the zoo.

Doctors and vets study poo to see how well an animal is digesting its food and to spot health problems. Some zoos are experimenting with using poo to produce bio-gas that can power vehicles or buildings – like a zoo hospital.

They pile some in towers
and toss it with rakes.

It soon will be compost
for gardeners to take.

Compost – made from herbivore poo mixed with food waste and grass clippings – improves soil and helps plants grow. Zoos sell or give away compost using creative names like Zoo Manoo, Zoo Doo, and Pachy Poo. Carnivore poo can be spread around yards to keep deer from eating plants and trees.

First, worms like to munch it,
and then we're all set!

For worm poo plus zoo poo
grows perfect courgettes!

Worms are an important part of the zoo-poo composting process. They can eat hundreds of kilograms of organic matter every week! Woodland Park Zoo in Seattle, USA sells Worm Doo, made from Zoo Doo compost and zoo coffee grounds. The zoo says, "It's been pooed once by exotic herbivores and pooed again by compost-loving worms."

They even make paper
from elephant poo.

Elephant poo comes out with so much plant fibre that a
machine can wash the poo and pull out the fibre, which
can then be used to make paper and cards.

Zoo-poo paper's pretty,
not smelly. It's true!

WHOA.

LOOK.

YIKES!

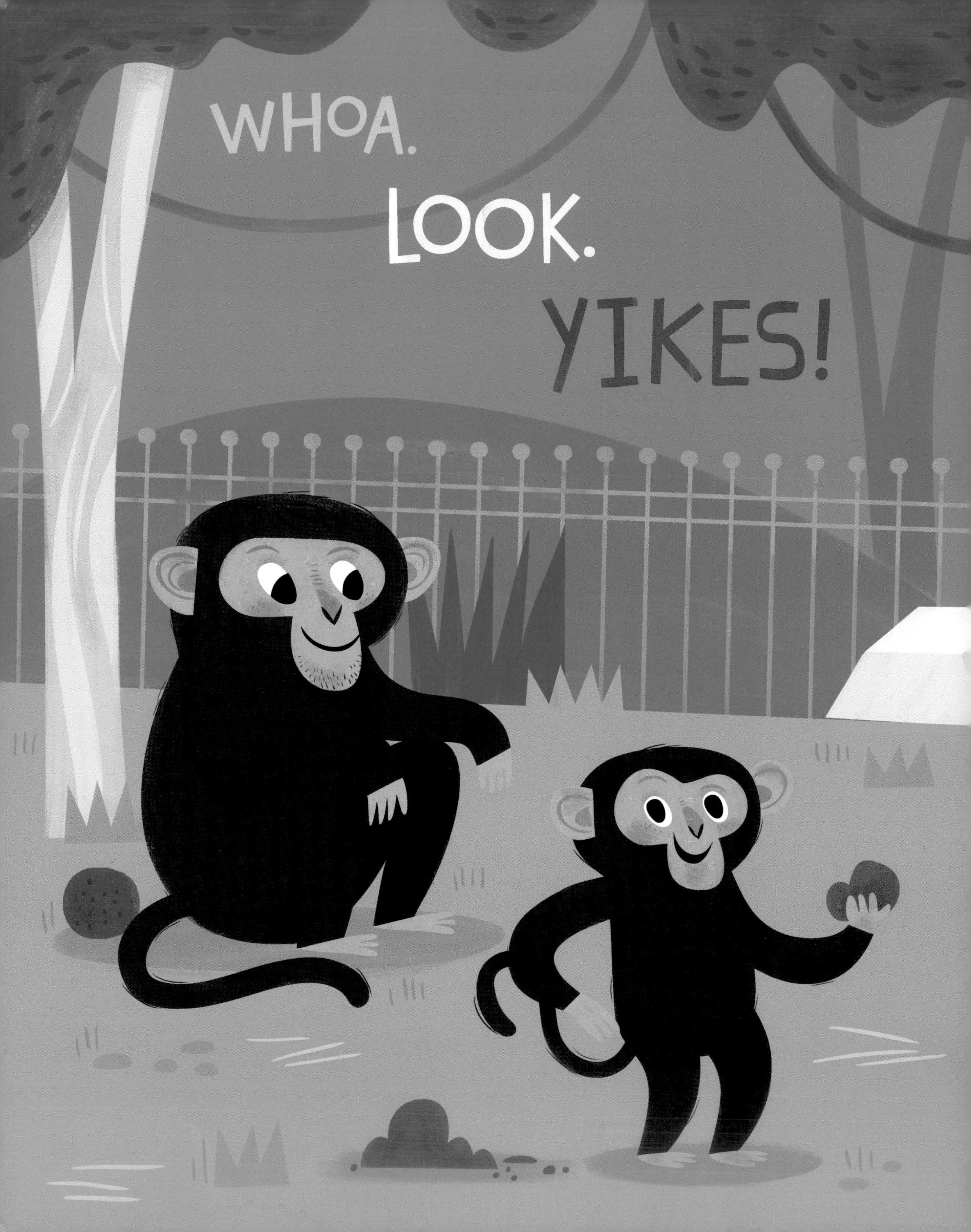

DUCK!

That monkey at the zoo . . .

Many primates throw poo. Scientists discovered that chimpanzees who throw the most poo and hit their target the most often are the smartest and most sociable, which suggests that throwing is a form of communication and self-expression – and maybe a step towards using tools.